A Mixtape of Mayhem © 2024 Nikki Ritchie

All rights reserved.

No part of this publication may be reproduced, stored in a retrieval system, or transmitted, in any form or by any means, electronic, mechanical, photocopying, recording or otherwise, without the prior written permission of the presenters.

Nikki Ritchie asserts the moral right to be identified as author of this work.

Presentation by *BookLeaf Publishing*

Web: www.bookleafpub.com

E-mail: info@bookleafpub.com

ISBN:9789358319996

First edition 2024

A Mixtape of Mayhem

Nikki Ritchie

India | USA | UK

ACKNOWLEDGEMENT

I would like to acknowledge the resilient spirits who danced with me through my life's mayhem—my beautiful Latvian, who held me tight during the chaos, my children, who held me steady during the storms, and my close family, who taught me the importance of resilience. I give a huge nod to all women who face menopause with grace and the wild souls who raved beside me in the moonlight all those years ago. Also, all those unknowns who inspired my poetic craziness and, of course, express gratitude to the readers who will join me in this lyrical journey.

PREFACE

In the musical of existence, where life notes crescendo and wane,
I invite you to a poetic mixtape, a songful refrain.

Here lies a journey, not for the faint of heart,
Through battles and menopause, where every line is a fresh start.

Midlife's dance floor, where craziness takes the lead,
With each verse, a testament to resilience indeed.

Feel the heat of the beats, the raving in your soul,
As we navigate the rhythm of life, making broken parts whole.

In the pages that follow, let the words sway and sing,
A mixtape of experiences, where emotions take wing.

So, dear reader, fasten your seatbelt tight,

For this poetic journey, through day and night.

May these verses resonate, a familiar tune,
In this mixtape of life, let us swoon.

Life's Resilience Disaster Dance

Life is full of sh*t-storms that appear without warning,
Given to you like a gift you'll soon be mourning.
In life's slapstick comedy, chaos takes the stage,
Disasters moonwalk, like an awkward dance engage.

Tripping on troubles, we stumble and sway,
Taking a jive through the calamity, come what may!
In the rhythm of the storm, we too take the floor,
Dancing through challenges, we seek to explore.
Tangos of resilience, or a graceful pirouette,
In each step, a solution we hope to get.

In life's tempest roar, a sh#t-storm finds its place,
They dance faster, with an unpredictable embrace.
Yet within the wreckage, seeds of strength are sown,
Resilience blooms, and our own spirit has grown.

The madness of the road

In the traffic's dance, there is a clumsy prance,
Stupid drivers, stuck in their own trance.
Left is right, and right is left,
In their world, all reason is inept.

On the asphalt stage, the human race begins,
Steering wheels and antics, where madness grins.
Indicators and clear minds forgotten, as if on vacation,
Driving manoeuvres, no thought for others, a strange coordination.

Speed demons fly past, like they're in a road race,
While turtles crawl, at a snail's gentle pace.

A horn beeping musical, a racket so grand,
In the car theatre play, mayhem takes command.

In the mist of road rage, tempers ignite,
Horns become angry voices in the traffic fight.
Frustration blooms like a flower untamed,
In the highway drama, sanity is named.

Steering wheel warriors, faces turn red,
In this comedy of madness, reason has fled.
Lane changers dance, in a waltz so bold,
GPS guiding, or so we're told.

But let's laugh it off, in this roadshow absurd,
For in the end, we're all just traffic nerds.

Es mīlu Tevi vairāk

Beneath the stars, destiny's sweet design,
I wandered through life, seeking a sign.
In the tapestry of fate, where moments entwine,
I found my soulmate, a love so divine.

Eyes met in a gaze, a connection so strong,
Two hearts drawn together, beating as one.
Through the madness of life, we found our way,
A love like ours will always stay.

In whispers of wind and the hush of the sea,
I heard echoes of love calling me.
My soulmate's connection, profound and free,
We sailed through the storms, just my love and me.

Hand in hand, we found the strength to get through,
In this crazy life of existence, our love deep and true.

Through laughter and tears, till the bad times were gone,
With my soulmate, together, we'll eternally bond.

My rock my strength, so thankful you came into my world,
Your kindness, beauty, an ineffable rare pearl.
A journey of love, of deep connections and fate,
I found my soulmate, and it was worth the wait.

I'm never drinking again....

In youth, we drank heavy without care,
Hangovers? We were blissfully unaware.
But as the years swiftly passed us by,
Hangovers became an unwelcome ally.

Once we could party until the dawn,
Now one too many, and for days we mourn.
The morning sun feels a bit too bright,
As we moan and swear we're done with that night.

In our prime, drinking crazy and bold,
Now a single drink or the idea leaves us feeling old.
The dance floor was our playground, so wild and free,
Now we ask, "Is it past 10 yet and I need a kebab, you see?"

Age and hangovers, an unexpected funny blend,

Reminders that time is our tricky old friend.
So, here's to the nights that we will never forget,
Now happier in my Jimmy jams and a dog to pet.

For now my excitement is a new series to binge,
Without the worry of a post night out cringe.
Memories of wild nights will stay with me forever,
Would I do it all again—never say never!

Me myself and I

In the mirror's gaze, a charmer's quest,
A narcissist, truly self-obsessed.
Ego soaring, like a spaceman's flight,
Reflections fuel their self-loving delight.

Persona beaming in perfection's grace,
Sickly smiles, an arrogant embrace.
Mirror, mirror on the wall,
Who's the greatest of them all?

Voices echo, "Me, myself, and I,"
An act full of lies beneath the sky.
In a world of one, they take their lead,
A narcissist's life story of greed.

But oh, the irony, a wonderful twist,
Their self-love often goes amiss.
For in their bubble, so pristine,
Comedy arises, a narcissist's scene.

The ego's throne begins to crack,
Reality delivers a sobering smack.
Reflections shattered, illusions break,
As the truth emerges, a quivering quake.

The lies unravel, a fleeting lover's kiss,
Old lovers and friends fade away in the abyss.
No more applause, no grand ovation,
Just echoes of self-adulation.

Alone they stand, no crowd to cheer,
The narcissist's end draws near.
Honesty shakes their head, a bitter friend,
As mirrors reflect a broken trend.

In the end, they cry a humbled plea,
A promise for change, for empathy.
But silence remains, a lesson learned,
As the narcissist's ego is finally spurned.

Memories of amazing trips

In the '90s, a rave was the crack,
Neon lights, and beats would smack.
Glow sticks swaying, a rhythmic dance,
Lost in daze, a techno trance.

Baggy jeans and oversized shirts,
UV paint, oh, the fashion got worse!
Flashing lights, a colour kaleidoscope,
Ecstasy pills, acid tabs, all providing hope.

Warehouse parties, secret gigs,
Eyes like saucers, mouth with a cig.
Pumping vibes, that was the call,
Hug a raver, embrace them all.

Goodies on hand to soothe the jaw,
Dancing free, no need for law.
The DJ's the god, the turntable alter,
Rave culture, the love—no one could fault her.

A time when glow was more than just sticks,
The love, the laughter and those amazing trips!
A time gone by, may never to repeat
A good job now, as my body needs a seat!

Menopause can do one

In the hell of menopause, a hot mess show,
Sweat cascades like a waterfall's flow.
Mood swings hit with an unfunny jest,
Emotional battles, put to the test.

Hot flashes erupt, a volcanic spree,
A sauna's envy, a performance to see.
Air-con shattered, it can't compete,
In this rude awakening, defeat is sweet.

Hormones mutiny with a rebel yell,
Turning tempers into a blazing hell.
Fans waft at pace in futile pride,
Against the inferno, they can't abide.

Menopause, the twat of a curse,
A life stage filled with chaos, just getting worse.
In this crap show of heat, sweat, moods and pain,
Laughs emerge, as a huge fart appears with no one to blame!

Cleaning, what a bore!

In the life of dust bunnies, a battle begins,
The vacuum roars, the mop twirls, the radio spins.
Dirty plates in rebellion, a drama unfolds,
Sponges and scrubbers, the sprays ahold.

The laundry pile, a mountain so high,
Socks playing hide-and-seek, oh my, you're so sly!
A dance with the mop, a fast paced jive,
Dust conspiracies, such a sneaky crime.

The latest spray in hand, mirrors beware,
Reflections scream, "That's not fair!"
Under the furniture, a lost trove of treasure,
Remote controls, and dreams of old pleasure.

In the cleaning quest, the house now gleams,
Floors so shiny, it sparkles in dreams.
But as one surface shines, another rebels,

A game of "shoes off!", "clean up after yourselves!"

So here's to the cleaners, the gold medalists of grime,
Life is too short, remember we're running out of time!
Leave those dishes, dust and wash day plan,
Spend time with your loved ones, do it while you can!

Shoes, shoes and more shoes

In the wardrobe kingdom, a shoe army is assembled,
Heels, trainers, a messy mountain resembled
Flip-flops for summer, boots for the snow,
A collection so vast, it continues to grow.... and grow.

Stilettos for glam, like towers so high,
I'm short, I need them, it is no lie.
Running shoes for speed, yeah right!
I might do it one day,.... I might!

Sandals for comfort, a breeze on each toe,
Each pair tells a tale, a footwear show.
No matter what your mood, or your look,
A beautiful shoe can get you hooked.

A rainbow of colours, a spectrum of delight,

All shapes and designs, I'm Imelda... alright!
Shoes make you happy, when all is unwhole,
They lift you in height and within your soul!

Wrinkles or Memories?

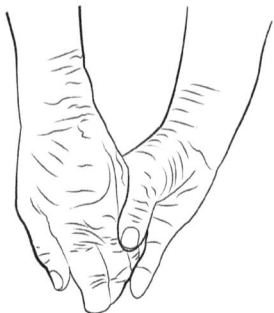

In the tapestry of time, a tale of saggy skin unfolds,
Wrinkles emerge, lines appear with tales to be told.
Age shows new lines on the face, each with a story,
Laughter leaves evidence of joy and worries in glory.

Crow's feet dancing, back and forth a show so bold,
A life well-lived, much laughter and jokes to be told.
Forehead full of furrows, deep like caverns unfold,
The years of adventures and fun, in wrinkles, it's scrolled.

Creases of wisdom, displayed on the brow,
A roadmap of moments, then and now.
Anti-aging creams, serums and gels a useless quest,
For in each and every wrinkle, life is expressed.

So here's to the laugh lines, the experience they bear,
In the grand story of time, wrinkles declare:
"We've recorded your years, like a well-worn song,
A memory of life, where wrinkles belong!"

Always my hero

In a head full of memories and pictures, my dad's voice I play,
His presence lingers in whispers, though he's now so far away.
Through the stages of life, his wisdom echoes like a song,
I hear his advice and antidotes sent lovingly and strong.

Gone, yet not forgotten, deep within my heart,
Dad's love and lessons linger, though we're worlds apart.
Whilst DIY or decorating chores, I feel his gentle gaze,
A whisper of advice, guiding me through life's maze.

My dad, my hero, my life's guiding light,
My strength and my power, my courage to fight.
He left this world but never my heart,
There he'll live forever, never to part.

A missed kind heart and wise words spoken,
A man well loved, left many heartbroken.
Fun instilled into life, with laughter and joy,
Especially with his favourites "our lassy" and "my boy"

A grave full of flowers and items for memorial,
We grieve, pay our respects—it's all material.
For dad lives within us and not at a graveside,
Memories of love replayed in our minds, with huge pride.

Dad, you will always be my hero.

Are you ignorant?

The beauty of the world is all around you,
Look deeper and closer, it's not brand new.
From nature, wonders of the world and human existence,
It was created long before mortals ran the distance.

Appreciate the planet, see it as your rental,
To be passed onto others, so be kind and gentle.
What you do now will impact generations,
Be remembered for exceeding expectations.

Recycle, reuse and cut down on waste,
Buy less plastic, not fill up landfill space.
Educate yourself and influence others,
Do it now, if not, we may never recover

Don't allow your ignorance and pride get in the way,
Saving our planet must be life every single day.
Protecting our planet starts with you today,
So change life and live in a sustainable way!

Shit, dick and rank

When life is full of shit, and everyone is a dick,
Your job is rank and you've no balance in the bank.
The lotto didn't pay out and your skin is mid-breakout.
The dog crapped in the house and the cat caught another mouse.

Don't despair, this is life, where problems are always rife!
Abstain from worry, chill out and let your stress go a flurry.
Pour the wine, or drink from the bottle, let the good times shine.

Eat what you want, order the takeaway…all nonchalant.

For we are not promised a tomorrow or a night bestow.
Live for today... let go, and feel the warm glow.
Kiss your loved ones, or anyone and everyone.
For we only live once, so enjoy the ride and let it slide!

I fought the bastard with all my might!

You creeped into my life and ripped it apart,
Tipped it upside down, broke my heart.
Shock caught my breath, anxiety stricken,
Flight mode activated and my heart quickens.

My life isn't over, I have so much to do,
Let me just find the strength to pull through.
I plead with those above to change my path,
To take away that evil bastard and its wrath.

Doctors words blurred and hazy,
My gaze must look like I'm crazy.
Flight mode engaged I run for the door,
Gliding across the hospital floor.

My sobs can be heard across the town,
"I'm not ready yet!" I shout out loud.
Anger fills my bones and boils my blood,
If this carries on I'll need to be drugged.

My world has collapsed around me,
Worry is all I can see.
How do I tell my kids what is found,
And that I might not be around.
Further tests and invasive procedures,
Blood tests taken, feels like litres!
Early stages, thankfully caught early,
I will do anything to continue my journey.

Suggested hysterectomy will remove every trace,
A decision is made and I do what it takes.
Recovery is slow, but I don't care or mind,
As long as I'm here to see what the future finds.

The months pass by and more tests are given,
Luckily all taken, passed and in good condition.
The five year all clear arrives with delight,
I fought the evil bastard with all my might!

Housework can wait

Did I miss the lesson on housework at school?
Was it on a Monday morning? And seen as uncool?
As I never did Mondays, or anything not happening,
So forgive me, parents, I may have been slacking.

I left home early, had to get my shit together,
Where housework was concerned, I didn't know better.
Decisions on laundry, meals and food shopping,
Who knew this part of adulting was so rocking.

Dusting, polishing, washing and hoovering,

Who knows what was what, honestly I knew nothing.
Bleach, sprays, powder or antibacterial,
It all costs a fortune and is all immaterial.

For over the years I've found my way,
Houses are clean and washing I slay.
But what matters in your life and mine,
Is living, not surviving so don't waste your time.

At the end of your life, will you reminisce,
About your time spent cleaning or memories of bliss.
Creating love or a sparkling abode,
Reminders of laughter or a home workload.

So ditch the duster and that dirty plate,
Enjoy your life, because housework can wait!

The King's of swagger

Cats are masters of disguise,
Fluffy cuteness with evil eyes.
They lure you in with purring sighs,
Whilst digging claws into your thighs.

King's of swagger, top of their game,
Expert mouse catcher, no-one to blame.
You wanna stroke me? I'll say when,
Under my chin, again and again.

Ignorance is their top trait,
Stolen chicken, not me mate!
Calling their name, only feet away,
I can't hear you, try another day.

Go off their food, whenever they like,
Careless about the cost of living hike.
Look you dead in the eye, no care considered,
I'll shit where I want, package delivered.

Cats chose you over any others,
So appreciate that you're now a mother.
They've loved you since a kitten,
Unless the neighbour offers real chicken!

Cheeeeeessse

Cheese is the food of gods,
The euphoric taste is the dogs.
Numerous regional variations,
Eclectic flavour sensations.

Too many to name,
Or favourites to claim.
Cheddar, edam, hallomi's the game,
They all deserve a claim to fame.

Melted, grated or sliced,
Smoked, infused or even spiced.
Specialist or highly priced,
I am so easily enticed.

Classic crackers, chutney and grapes.

On toast, a sandwich or in a crepe.
Pasta, mash, pizza and salad,
Cheese is my love song ballad.

Baby Busters

In a generation of our old fashioned parents,
And new age, forward, diverse adolescents.
Social media, green and diversity now lead the way,
Versus dance halls, written letters and strict parents in their day.

Expectations of marriage, children and a successful career,
Was the rule book of life that must be followed all clear.
Today we celebrate diversity and inclusion, free speech,
Giving everyone rights to expression and freedom to preach.

My generation X straddles and braces the in-between,
A time of shifting values and things not quite as they seem.
New technology to learn and strong social identities to yearn.

We adapted to changes and even Bobby Ewing's return.

Latchkey kids labelled the MTV generation,
Defined by Conservativism and the franchise mega-sequel situation.
Endured recessions, and those damn rotary dial telephones,
We are resilient, fiercely independent and can be left home alone!

So being the bridge between boomers and millennials,
Is nothing to us as we're bloody hardy perennials!

Make it do one

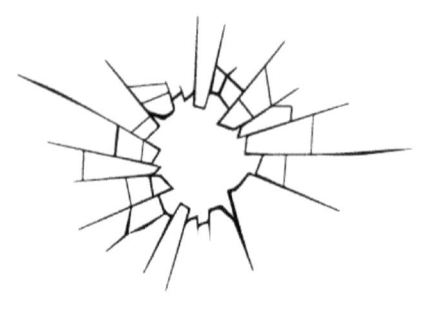

Difficulty breathing, panic, fatigue sweeping,
Chest pains, headache, sore eyes weeping.
Blurred vision, blindspots, tension creeping.
Overwhelmed, anxious, heartbeat leaping.

Racing thoughts day and night,
Concentration gone, chest so tight,
Negative thoughts, unable to fight,
Anxiety sky high, can't see the light.

Mental anguish and physical ills,
Relaxation and popping pills.
It's closing in on you, losing the will.
Change, get help, you know the drill.

Nervous system damage, beyond repair,
High blood pressure, needs medical care.
Heart strained, injured, in disrepair,
Family in turmoil, had a scare.

Stress can change you, that can't be undone,
It can ruin your life, even have you gone.
Hold your loved ones tight, use them to lean on,
Alter your habits, take control and let stress do one!

Lalizig

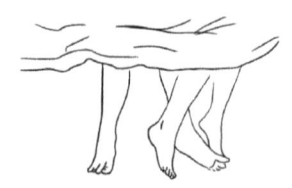

I saw you and felt immediate connection,
It was in that moment I felt the affection,
Your beauty and radiance gave me the flutters,
But attempts to express my love leave me in stutters.

I adore every piece of you and melt when you're around,
You make my world shine and my loving heart pound.
If I could, I would give you everything you deserve,
The wonder you bring into my life I'm happy to serve.

Time is slipping away, so let's take the chance,
Put all of our love and passion into this romance.
I'll risk it all if it means being with you,
Time spent together is all I'm happy to do.

You're all I need and all that I want in my life expedition,

Can't you see that you're my one and only mission.
You make me feel like I'm on a massive trip of highs,
With the look of love from your beautiful brown eyes.

I undress you in my mind everytime I see you,
Your shape is so divine, I need a sneak preview,
Sometimes I get drawn to others and my eyes wander,
But it's always you I return to and want to conquer.

Your taste is beyond compare; silky texture sickly sweet,
The sugar high makes me want to yell—repeat, repeat!
When I take you in my grasp, palpitations start to hit,
My shaky hand as I undress your each and every bit.

The first mouthful is a drug rush I will always crave,
It hits the spot deep down, I am your slave...
The addiction is strong and I cannot go on,
Without my chocolate bar to munch upon!

To be brave

Is it the right time to take that chance,
Will I ever get to celebrate and dance?
Can I reach my longed for goal,
Or will it laugh and destroy my soul.

Scared to risk in all that is achieved,
To cross the bridge of risk to succeed.
Dare I push my boundaries open wide,
Break those tethered shackles of pride.

Will I ever emerge from the other side,
It could be a tough journey and a lonely ride.

But I'm told it will be worth the pain,
To feel me again and clear the rain.

To take that first step is my own battle,
One that I must find the strength to tackle.
For to live a life of pain and lies,
Is one I do not deserve or compromise.

Strength building and confidence improving,
I can see the light and the darkness reducing.
It's coming through loud and clear,
I need to empower myself to get out of here!

Mixtape Madness

In the tape deck world, a bygone age
I set out on a quest, a musical stage
With buttons that click and dials that turn
I embark on a journey, a mixtape churn

Radio waves dance in the broadcasting air
As I fumble with controls, a funny affair
Static and glitches, like a naughty sprite
In this analog adventure, it is pure delight

Recording pauses, a tough strategic game
As songs on the radio play hide and claim
Fingers crossed, hoping the DJ won't speak
In this mixtape making, my stress level peaks

Unravelled tangled tapes, like spaghetti strands
A song full of chaos, crafted by my own fair hands
But oh, the joy in each quirky mistake

In this tape deck tale, memories awake

Fast forward, rewind, a time-travel spree
In the land of mixtapes, where humour runs free
From cassette to cassette, a crafted race
A radio fueled contest, in this nostalgic space.

Adult children, when did that happen?

In the realm of adulthood, my children now roam
A wild journey, that was loved and feels like home
They've grown so fast, a frenzied race
From tiny footprints to a bustling pace

Love them, I do, with a pride filled heart
As they navigate life, each unique part
Their stories and tales, a source of delight
Memories to be made, any day or night

They have wonderful lives, interesting and fun
Full of surprises, each and every one
In their unique ways, they bring joy and cheer
I cherish them deeply, year after year

From childhood antics to adult glee
A wonderful bond, my cup of tea
Their traits and charms, a beautiful and vibrant blend
Loving my adult children, always and forever—my best friends

Chihuahua

In a world of tiny paws and attitude delight
Chihuahua's pony prance is a comical sight
With ears that stand like antennae so high
Pocket sized jesters, reaching for the sky

In the morning sun, they proudly patrol
Tiny soldiers on a quest for a stroll
Their voices may be small, but oh they're bold
My Chi Chi's, the leaders of antics untold

A miniature parade, with tails held high
In their world, everyday's a party nearby
They strut with sass, a confident dance
Leaving a trail of laughter in their wake, by chance

We love our Chi Chi's, the fun they bring
With every tiny hop, every curious fling

In this world of big pooches and fashionable breeds
Chihuahua's reign supreme, in our world they succeed!

Don't let them get me!

The journey we take after a break up in life,
Is rough and hard, causing so much strife,
It chews you up and spits you out,
Leaving you feeling in a terrible clout.

I am told that there is light far into the distance
Although getting there is a feat of existence
The days are long and hard, feelings so intense
Will the old you reappear or just leave you in suspense

The eyes take the toll of hardened abuse
Those red flags you witnessed were no excuse
Behaviour so evil and raw, but so unaware
A blind eye was given through a begged prayer

A raw hope of change was left in despair
The look of the devil was in their wicked stare
Dare to speak or offered opinion was thwarted

Your thoughts and events often seem distorted

Their lies believed only by themselves, seeds all sown
A tale of untruths and deceit, but only their own
The blatant and openness of covering their tracks
Telling everyone who'll listen, they are being attacked

The secrets, misbehaviours and second lives are true
They're outwardly caring, telling others their view
But it's all an act, just a cover to continue their abuse
In a world that is lived only their way—no excuse!

You know you need to fight and break the painful cycle
But they're in this to destroy you and fully in denial
Living this life so hard, you can barely function
Giving your all in this relationship dysfunction

Let's hope for the day that karma takes the stage
To rid this evil person of their illness and rage
For those closest get hurt, damaged and defiled

By the behaviour and words of a devil so vile

It will get worse before it gets better, they say
But living is far better than dying, in any such way
Get help, find your inner voice, or just pray to a divine being
Just don't let them take your life, your soul or wellbeing!

The job hunt

In the kingdom of job hunts, I reign supreme,
Master of Netflix, the ultimate dream
Suited and booted? Nah, it's pyjamas all day
Unemployment chic, that's my runway.

LinkedIn updates just creative fiction
My skills include napping and Tiktock addiction
Interviews? I schedule them in my sleep
Dreaming of job offers, oh, the company I keep

The alarm clock protests, a wasted shout
I'm on my own schedule, that's what it's all about.
Latte is my coworker, the kitchen my desk
Unemployment perks, I must confess

Interview rejection? A badge I wear proud
Unemployment's my canvas, laughter my shroud

In this battle to find work, I take the lead
Jobless and thriving, that's all I need

"The right one will come your way" is all I hear,
Recruiters on tap, with job promises so sincere.
Claims given they've found the perfect role for you
100 miles away and half the wage you're used to

1st, 2nd and 3rd interviews attended
Presentations given and cv amended
But no such luck in this mad and crazy job pursuits
I guess it's back to standing in that bloody lottery queue!

Ok I'm a little round

In a world of salads and exercise pursuits,
I navigate life eating dust and fruits
My shadow's a bit on the rounder side
But who needs six-pack abs for this life's ride?

Cheese and chips, my trusted allies
In a battle of bulge, they win first prize
Running late? Well, I waddle with pride
A penguin on a mission, wobbling side to side.

Fashion's a challenge, sizes don't align
But hey, my wardrobe just needs a little redesign
Button poppin', seam stretchin', fabric array
My clothes scream, "It's a stretchy pants kinda day!"

Weightlifting? Sure, I lift carbs to my face
A workout routine in the food court space
I'm not heavy; I'm just gravity's muse
An earthly marvel with extra cruise.

So, here's to the joy in every belly roll
In a world obsessed, let laughter take control.
Life's too short for a size-based debate
I'm happy inside and loving my own weight!

Hell, to earn a living

In the workplace shadows where toxicity creeps,
Silent whispers poison, as morale weeps
Clocking in, but not just for the pay
Drowning in the toxic workday

Meetings, a deception of deceit,
Smiling masks, concealing the heat
Backstabbing whispers in the canteen air
A toxic dance, a workplace affair.

Gossip spreads like wildfire's flame
Blame and shame, the unending game
The air is heavy with stress and despair
In the toxic office, no one is spared

But in this darkness, resilience may bloom
A strength that rises, dispelling the gloom
Hold your head high, though the environment's grim,
For toxic storms eventually grow dim

If all is lost and your work life balance is unfair
Use your strength and get the hell out of there!

Finding life again

In the quiet corners where shadows fade,
A tale unfolds of a life remade.
Once lost in the labyrinth of despair,
Now arises a soul, free from the snare.

Through the ruins of dreams, a phoenix rises,
Shedding the ashes of any past disguises
In the grand picture of time, a fresh beginning
A journey of rediscovery, a life to start living

The heart, once heavy with burdens untold
Finds new beats, new lyrics, a rhythm bold.
The echoes of pain, now distant cries
As hope rekindles, like morning skies

Footsteps faltered in the chasm so deep
Now dance with purpose, no longer asleep
Among the stars, a constellation reborn

In the cosmic sky, a new life to adorn.

Through the whispers of wind and rivers' flow,
A rejuvenated spirit and soul begin to grow
Among the wreckage, appear seeds of change
A metamorphosis, so beautifully strange.

From the cocoon of sorrow, emerges a butterfly
A sign of resilience and beauty, flying high
New chapters written, with vibrant revelation
In the tale of life, a rebirth, and transformation.

In the beauty of change, colours anew
A palette of happiness, where dreams can come true
The story of growth, the dance of fate
In the rediscovery of life, a celebration awaits.

So, in the magic of time, I find my way
Crafting a destiny, bright as day
For in the art of life, a living to regain
A being rekindled; I need it now—it's my time to reign!

Baltic Love

In the Baltic embrace, where amber gleams,
Latvia unfolds, a land filled with dreams.
Among pine-clad forests and amber-lit shore
A tale of resilience, a place I simply adore

Riga, the jewel with spires that stand tall
A city's heartbeat, a beauty loved by all.
Cobbled streets echo stories untold
Of historic tales, in brick and gold

Jūrmala's beaches, where the Baltic winds sigh
Within dunes and pines, where seagulls fly high
A canvas of amber, on the shore's dance floor
Nature and history in a beautiful sweet outpour

Sigulda's whispers through vast castle walls,
A medieval tapestry where adventure calls
Land of folk songs, where voices entwine
Daina's resonance, a magical cultural shrine.

Through harvests and hardships, a resilient song
Latvia's spirit, so resilient and strong.
Among beautiful lakes and Eastern grace
An Orthodox embrace, in a tranquil space

Latvia's seasons, a visual and sensory delight,
From winter's frost to hot summers so bright.
In the amber glow of a Latvian eye,
A nation's spirit, you cannot deny.

A Reason for living

Beneath the vast heavenly dome
A quest unfolds, a journey to roam
In the art of time, threads untwine,
A search for purpose, a destiny to define

Through fields of doubt and mountains of strife
We tread the path to discover our life.
In the maze of choices, a winding trail
Each step is growth, a progressive tale.

The canvas of being, blank and vast
The colours of moments, future and past
Seeking purpose, finding a flame within
Igniting the soul, where dreams begin

In the heart's echo, a subtle call
A purpose profound, waiting to enthral
A story of passion, with notes untold,
A melody crafted in dreams' stronghold.

Through trials and errors, we navigate
In the narrative of life, destinies congregate
The purpose, a beacon, distant and bright
Guiding us through the darkest night.

It may emerge in dreams or artistic creation
A mission unfolding, a divine revelation
For some, it's written in signs of care
In kindness bestowed, a purpose so rare

In the pursuit of knowledge or love's embrace
We unravel the story, we find our place
A purpose discovered, not glory quests
But in the simple moments, where ikigai invests

So, let the journey unravel, let purpose unfold,
In the stories written, in destinies told
For in each heartbeat, in every forgiving
We discover our purpose, a reason for living!

A sacred heart yearns

In shadows cast by the setting sun
A grief unfolds, a sorrow begun.
A heart once whole, now shattered, torn
In the wake of loss, a loved soul forlorn

Whispers of memories, echoes so clear
A symphony of joy, now drowned in tears
The laughter, the warmth, like a fleeting mist
Gone in an instant, a love sadly missed

Silent footsteps echo in empty halls
The absence of presence, a sorrow that befalls
A vacant chair, a lingering smell
A void so deep, in grief we dwell

Through tear-streaked windows, the world looks grey
As the sun refuses to brighten the day.

The clock's relentless ticking, a cruel decree
Marking the passage of time without thee

In dreams, you linger, a bittersweet waltz
A dance with a loved one, in memory's vaults
The ache of loss, an eternal sea
Where waves of grief crash relentlessly
Yet, amid sorrow, a flicker of light,
A constellation of love, piercing the night
For though you've departed, your spirit lives on,
In every sunrise, every dusk, until dawn.

So, within these words, a heartache confessed
A time full of grief, in sorrow, dressed.
Yet, through the tears, love's ember shall burn
In the sacred heart where memories yearn

Music, my drug of choice

Music has the power to lift, soothe and inspire
Calm your nerves or raise you up like fire
Strings that weep, and beats that talk
A musical language felt in every walk

From soaring heights to depths untold
A journey of musical notes unfolds
In rhythm's grip, all hearts entwine
Music, the drug, so divine

In the land where notes dance and play
A witty tale, so let me convey
A composition of laughter, a rhythm so grand
Music's showcase, a banging band

First, the bass, a lowly jest
Tickling your senses, a musical quest
It rumbles deep, a mischievous game
Shaking your soul, never the same

Then arrives the treble, a cheeky sprite
Feelings evoke, oh, what delight!
It dances high, like a misbehaving breeze
Leaving you raving, weak in the knees

The melody grows, beats pump like rap
Swirling you 'round in its rhythmic trap
Feelings soar and rush, like a waterfall's glee
Music's embrace, a soulful spree.

But beware the key changes, a mischievous twist
A musical prank, you can't resist.
Your heart skips a beat, caught by surprise
Oh, the high that music implies!

So, let the chords jest, let the rhythms tease
In the rave of sound, let your soul release
For in this melody, a drug rush appeal
Music's laughter is truly surreal

We knew it all…didn't we?

In times of our youth, we have grand ideas
No need for study, or eating healthy—just love for Tia Maria's!
Who has the time to think and consider later life
When partying, alcohol and substances were rife

Raves, dancing and friends were the priority
Not careers, pensions and damn conformity
You'd live for today, enjoying the moment
Standing up for now becoming your own proponent

No consequences were thought, or considered
No-one realised the danger of a life embittered
Life was hard for the rents, that wasn't my future
We wanted forever young, not to become some old loser!

How times have changed, looking back on our youth
Great memories were made, best times was our truth
Although life may have been easier if we took more notice
But we knew better, at the time it landed on the hopeless

We didn't do too bad, those that made it through
And who really listened, and took advice from an older crew
In youthful minds, the truth did gleam
We knew it all, or so we'd dream!

Beautiful double

In times of trouble, you are there, beaming bright
You build my strength to push on and fight the fight
You bring me love in a way I cannot ever explain
Without you my world would be full of hate and pain

I thank you for giving me the confidence to grow
In times when I thought bad thoughts, they just wouldn't go
You light up my life and my heart deep inside
The beauty you radiate both in and out, is undenied

I love the way you look at me and I feel such inner peace

A bond so strong, unbreakable and never to cease
We are written in the stars; fate made our connection strong
How can we question something where I know we belong

We were pulled together by a hypnotic strength, so intense
The power you exude creates a love and passion, it's immense
You understand me like nobody else, you're under my skin
A medium could not compete with your feeling, my head is all a spin

Forever is where I want to be with you, my world is empty if we can't be two
How lucky we are to have a love so real; I love you the way you make me feel
The pledge we share, is beyond compare, making the perfect pair
We're happy being in our bubble, just us, our beautiful double.

Milton Keynes UK
Ingram Content Group UK Ltd.
UKHW021041020824
446373UK00014B/564